Energy Essentials
Nuclear Energy

Nigel Saunders and Steven Chapman

Raintree

For information, address the publisher:
Raintree, 100 N. LaSalle, Suite 1200, Chicago, IL 60602

Printed and bound in China
10 09 08 07 06
10 9 8 7 6 5 4 3 2 1

Library of Congress Cataloging-in-Publication Data

Saunders, N. (Nigel)
    Nuclear energy / Nigel Saunders and Steven Chapman.
      p. cm. -- (Energy essentials)
    Includes bibliographical references and index.
    ISBN 1-4109-1694-4 (library binding-hardcover) --
    ISBN 1-4109-1699-5 (pbk.) 1. Nuclear engineering--Juvenile
    literature. I. Chapman, Steven. II. Title. III. Series.

    TK9148.S2856 2005
    333.792'4--dc22

                                            2005003642

This leveled text is a version of Freestyle: Energy Essentials: Nuclear
Energy.

Acknowledgments
pp.**4/5**, Photodisc; p.**4**, Tudor Photography; p.**5**, (top) Science
Photo Library/Chris Butler; p.**5**, (middle) Science Photo Library;
p.**5**, (bottom) Science Photo Library; p.**6**, (top) Photodisc; p.**6**,
(bottom) Corbis; p.**7**, Science Photo Library/U.S. Dept. of Energy;
pp.**8–9**, Science Photo Library; p.**8**, Science Photo Library; p.**10**,
Photodisc; p.**11**, Science Photo Library; p.**12**, (top) Illustrated
London News; p.**12**, (bottom) Science Photo Library/David Parker;
p.**13**, (top) Science Photo Library; p.**13**, (bottom) Corbis; p.**14**,
Science Photo Library; p.**15**, (top) National Air and Space
Museum, Smithsonian Institute; p.**15**, (bottom) Science Photo
Library; pp.**16/17**, Getty Images; p.**16**, Science Photo Library;
p.**17**, Science Photo Library; pp.**18/19**, Science Photo Library;
p.**18**, Science Photo Library; p.**19**, Rex Features/ Stock Medical;
p.**20**, (top) Science Photo Library; p.**21**, Science Photo
Library/Scott Camzine; pp.**22/23**, Corbis; p.**22**, Corbis; p.**23**,
Photodisc; p.**24** (right) Corbis/ Tim Wright; p.**24**, (left) Corbis;
pp.**26/27**, Science Photo Library; p.**26** Corbis; p.**27**, Australia
Picture Library; p.**28**, (top) Science Photo Library; p.**28**, (bottom)
Science Photo Library; p.**29**, Science Photo Library/Volker Steger;
pp.**30/31**, U.S. Navy Visual News Service/ James Thierry; p.**30**,
Corbis; p.**31**,Corbis; p.**33**, Science Photo Library; pp.**34/35**,
Corbis; pp.**34**, Corbis; p.**35**, PA Photos/EPA; p.**36**, (top) Science
Photo Library; p.**36**, (bottom) Science Photo Library; p.**37**, Corbis;
p.**38**, Photodisc; p.**39**, NASA/HSTI; p.**40**, Science Photo Library;
pp.**40/41**, PA Photos; p.**41**, Corbis; p.**42**, Corbis; p.**43**, (top) p.**43**,
(bottom) Corbis; pp.**44/45**, Science Photo Library.

Cover photograph of Tokamak plasma reproduced with
permission of Science Photo Library

Every effort has been made to contact copyright holders of any
material reproduced in this book. Any omissions will be rectified
in subsequent printings if notice is given to the publishers.

Disclaimer:
All the Internet addresses (URLs) given in this book were valid at
the time of going to press. However, due to the dynamic nature of
the Internet, some addresses may have changed, or sites may have
changed or ceased to exist since publication. While the author and
Publishers regret any inconvenience this may cause readers, no
responsibility for any such changes can be accepted by either the
author or the Publishers.

Contents

Any words appearing in the text in bold, **like this**, are explained in the Glossary. You can also look out for some of them in the Word bank at the bottom of each page.

What is Energy?

Have you ever read "Gives you **energy!**" on the side of a cereal box? Scientists say that energy is "being able to do work." Energy is what enables you to get up in the morning, get dressed, and walk to school.

Energy comes in many forms. Heat, sound, and light are three forms of energy. In this book you are going to find out about another form of energy called nuclear energy.

Energy from food

Food contains energy. When we eat food we use the energy in it. This helps us to speak, work, move, and grow.

Word Store   energy   being able to do work. Light, heat, and electricity are types of energy.

Fuels

We get energy from **fuels**. Fuels store energy. Energy is stored in fuels such as wood, coal, and gas. When the fuel is burned, the energy is turned into heat and light energy.

Nuclear energy comes from a different kind of fuel.

▼ Lightning contains huge amounts of energy.

Find out later ...

. . . *what this machine does.*

. . . *how* **radiation** *affects living things.*

. . . *what happens when a* **nuclear reactor** *explodes.*

fuel   substance that stores energy and releases it when it is burned

Radiation

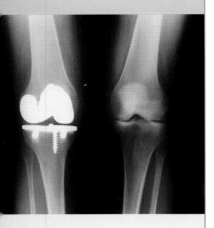

X-rays

X-rays are a type of radiation. This X-ray photograph shows the metal plate inside an artificial knee joint.

We can sense most kinds of **energy**. We can see light energy, hear sound energy, and feel heat energy. But there are some forms of energy that we cannot see, hear, or feel.

Invisible energy

Think of the the radio waves that bring music to our ears. We cannot feel or see them. Think of microwave ovens. They cook using invisible energy. This invisible energy is called **radiation**. Nuclear energy is also a form of radiation.

▼ The scientists Marie and Pierre Curie did many experiments with radiation.

Word Store radiation type of energy in the form of rays, waves, or particles

Radioactivity

Some rocks and metals release invisible radiation energy. This invisible radiation energy is called radioactivity. Materials that give off this energy are said to be **radioactive**.

We can use some of these radioactive materials to make nuclear energy.

▼ This lump of radioactive metal gives off lots of radiation energy. This makes it glow in the dark.

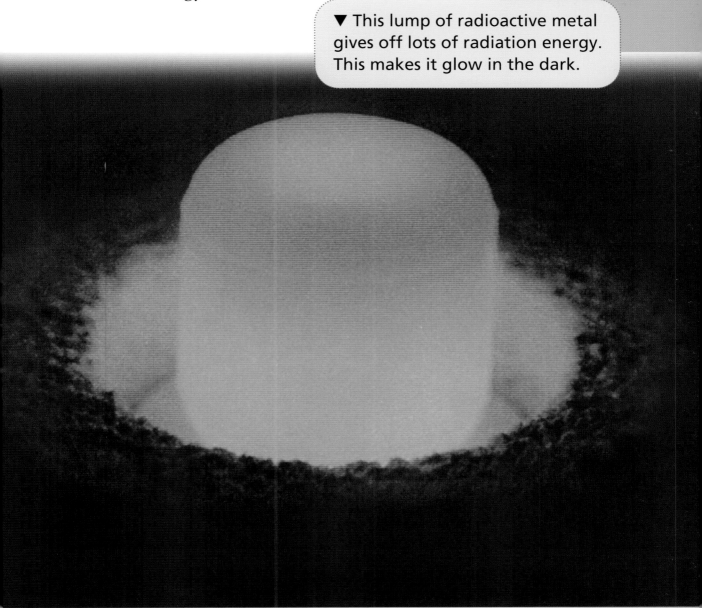

Atoms

Everything around us is made from very tiny **particles** called **atoms**. Even you are made of atoms!

There are over a hundred different types of atoms. All of them are much too small for us to see.

▲ Each of these substances is made from a different type of atom.

▶ This image is made by a special microscope. It shows some gold atoms on top of some carbon atoms.

Word Store   atom   tiny particle. Everything is made from atoms.

Subatomic particles

Atoms are made up of even smaller particles called **subatomic particles** (see diagram, right).

The center of an atom is called the **nucleus**. Whizzing around the nucleus are particles called **electrons**.

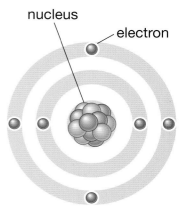

nucleus

electron

▲ This is a picture of a carbon atom.

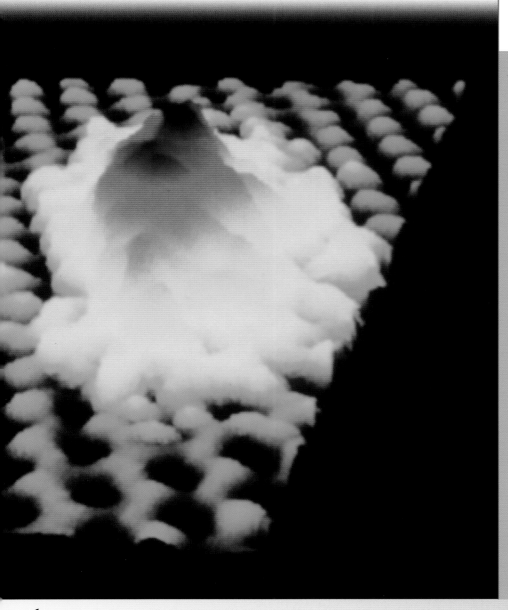

Nuclear energy

The **nucleus** of an atom can be split apart. When this happens, an enormous amount of **energy** is released.

This is what we call nuclear energy. It is called *nuclear* energy because it comes from the *nucleus* of an atom.

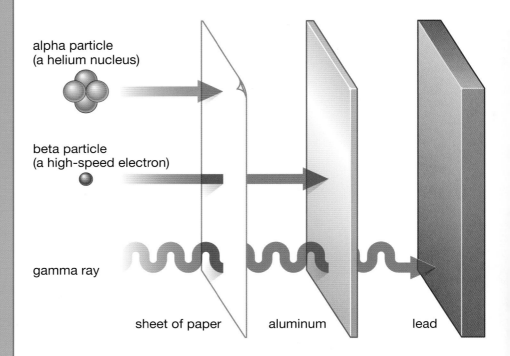

alpha particle
(a helium nucleus)

beta particle
(a high-speed electron)

gamma ray

sheet of paper   aluminum   lead

▲ These are the three main types of radiation. They can all travel through air but are stopped by different substances.

Most atoms do not break apart on their own. But scientists can make some atoms break into smaller pieces.

When the **nuclei** of these atoms are broken up, nuclear energy is given out in the form of **radiation**.

◄ These scientists are checking levels of radiation.

nuclei   more than one nucleus

Nuclear Energy

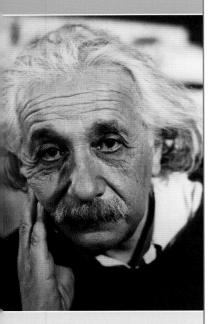

Albert Einstein

The scientist Albert Einstein warned scientists not to use nuclear energy for making weapons.

Splitting atoms

Splitting **atoms** is not easy. Scientists use large machines called **particle accelerators** to split atoms. They fire **particles** at very high speeds into atoms. This makes them break apart.

▼ This machine is a particle accelerator. It is used to get particles moving at high speeds.

Word Store   particle accelerator   machine that speeds up subatomic particles to very high speeds

Nuclear reactions

Splitting the atom is a type of **nuclear reaction**. In nuclear power stations, nuclear reactions are used to make electricity.

We can then use the electricity in many different ways.

▼ This is a nuclear power station in Illinois.

nuclear reaction   reaction that changes the nucleus of an atom

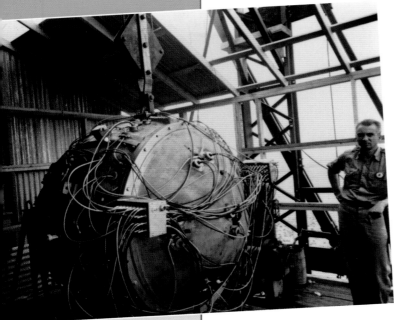

Nuclear fission

The splitting of atoms in this way is called **nuclear fission**. The word fission means "breaking apart."

To make nuclear **energy**, scientists have to shoot **particles** at very high speeds into **atoms** of a metal called **uranium**. The **nucleus** breaks up into two smaller **nuclei**.

Nuclear bombs

Scientists have used nuclear energy to make atomic bombs. This bomb was tested in New Mexico, USA, in 1945.

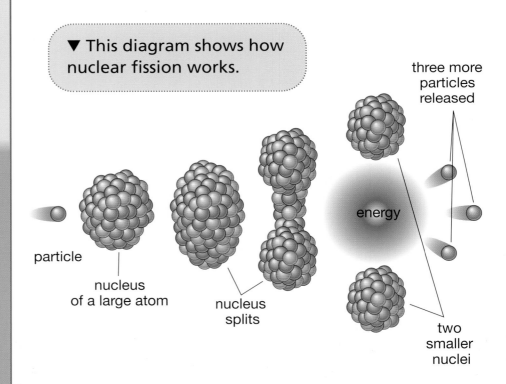

▼ This diagram shows how nuclear fission works.

particle

nucleus of a large atom

nucleus splits

energy

three more particles released

two smaller nuclei

Chain reactions

When the nucleus splits, more particles shoot out. These particles crash into other nuclei and split them up. This happens again and again in a process called a **chain reaction**.

Scientists can use a chain reaction to make nuclear energy. But they have to be careful. If the reaction happens too fast, it could cause a nuclear explosion.

War with atomic bombs

Hiroshima in Japan (above) was destroyed by an atomic bomb. It was dropped by the US during World War Two.

◀ This huge fireball was made by the world's first atomic bomb. It was tested in 1945.

chain reaction   nuclear reaction that keeps itself going

Radioactivity

▲ This device is used to measure radiation levels.

Radioactive substances are all around us. They give out **radiation** all the time. This is called background radiation.

Radon

Has your house ever been checked for radon? Radon is a radioactive gas. It comes from the **uranium** in rocks. Radon can seep into houses. People can get help to stop it getting into their homes.

How much background radiation you are exposed to depends on where you live, your job, and what you eat. This pie chart shows where background radiation comes from.

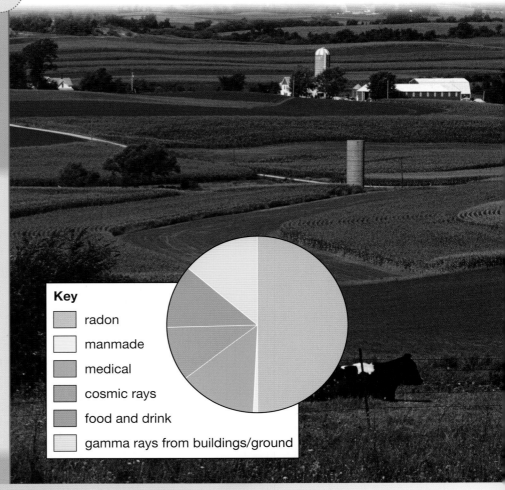

Key
- radon
- manmade
- medical
- cosmic rays
- food and drink
- gamma rays from buildings/ground

Word Store   uranium   radioactive metal used as a fuel

Radioactivity in food

Radioactive substances in the soil can pass into plants and animals. When humans eat these they take in a bit of radioactivity too. But don't worry, the amount of radioactivity is very small.

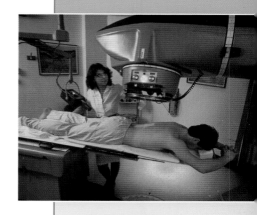

Cosmic rays

Another source of natural radiation is cosmic **rays** from space. Luckily, most of these never reach us on Earth.

Checking radiation

Some people have jobs that could expose them to dangerous levels of radiation. They have to have regular checks to show they are healthy.

ray   beam of light or radiation

Radiation and living things

Our bodies are made up of tiny parts called **cells**. If we are exposed to **radiation** it can damage our cells.

DNA damage

Radiation can damage the **DNA** inside our cells. DNA is a chemical that carries all the information that cells need to work properly. If the DNA is damaged by radiation, cells can develop wrongly or die.

Fly damage

This fruit fly has two pairs of wings instead of one. This has happened because the fly was exposed to radiation.

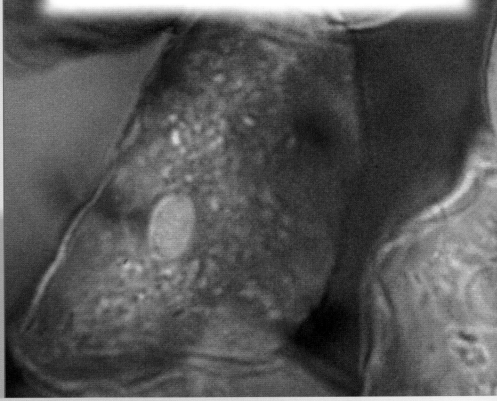

Word Store   DNA   chemical that carries information that cells need to work properly

Radiation from the Sun

Sunshine contains a type of radiation called **ultraviolet radiation**. Ultraviolet rays are invisible.

Our skin turns darker to protect us from the ultraviolet rays. This is what we call a tan. A tan is a sign that our skin is damaged. Too much sunbathing can cause skin **cancer**.

▼ Living things are made from cells. These are cells from the inside of a cheek, seen with a microscope.

Sunbathing
It is important to wear a sunscreen when you are out in the sunshine.

Nuclear medicine

Radiation is used a lot in medicine. **Radioactive** substances called tracers can be used to check the body for diseases. Different tracers travel to different parts of the body. They may go to the bones, heart, brain, or kidneys.

The tracers give off weak **rays** that are easily picked up by a scanner but do not harm the patient.

Tracers

The scan above was made using radioactive tracers. It shows two healthy kidneys.

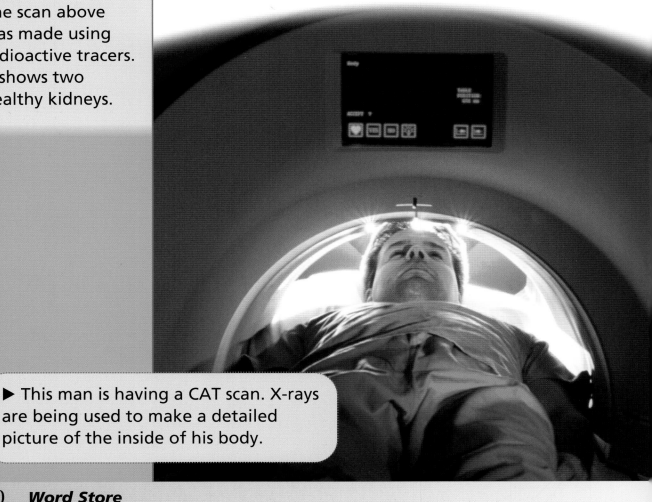

▶ This man is having a CAT scan. X-rays are being used to make a detailed picture of the inside of his body.

Treating cancer

Radiation can damage the **DNA** in **cells** so that they grow out of control. This is what causes the disease **cancer**.

However, because radiation can destroy cells, it can be used to treat cancer by killing the cancer cells.

▲ Food can be treated with radiation to kill harmful **bacteria**. This symbol means that the food has been treated with radiation.

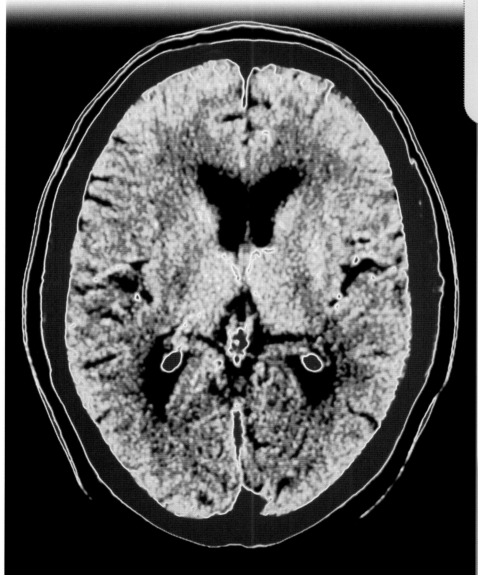

CAT scans

A CAT scan takes a picture of a "slice" through the body. It does this by sending a lot of weak X-rays through the body. This CAT scan (left) shows the inside of a person's brain.

cancer   disease caused by cells growing out of control

Energy from Heat

Power stations are where electricity is produced. Electricity is produced by using heat **energy** to make steam to turn **turbines**. These turn **generators** that make electricity.

Fossil fuels

Most power stations use one of the **fossil fuels**: coal, oil, or natural gas. These are burned to boil water and make steam.

Hot baths

Sometimes the hot water in the ground comes to the surface as springs. This is the Roman bath at Bath in the UK (above).

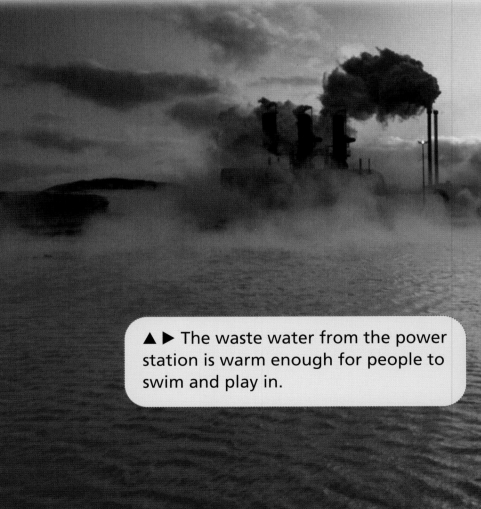

▲ ▶ The waste water from the power station is warm enough for people to swim and play in.

turbine   machinery that is turned by moving air, water, or steam

Hot rocks

Heat is given out by the **radioactive** substances in rocks deep inside the Earth. In some places these hot rocks heat water underground to boiling point.

The heat energy in rocks is called **geothermal** energy. Geothermal power stations use the energy from hot rocks to make electricity.

Geysers

Hot water underground can come to the surface as a hot jet of water and steam. This is called a geyser. The picture below shows the Old Faithful geyser in Yellowstone National Park.

The first nuclear reactor

The first nuclear reactor was called Chicago Pile 1. Part of it can be seen below. It was built at the University of Chicago in 1942.

Making nuclear power

In nuclear power stations the heat for making steam is provided by **nuclear fission**. When **atoms** are split in this way, a lot of heat **energy** is produced. This is what makes nuclear power.

The nuclear reactor

Inside a nuclear power station is a machine called a **nuclear reactor**. The **fuel** is a type of **uranium**.

The nuclear reactor (right) is surrounded by a strong concrete shield. This stops **radiation** leaking out. Inside it is the steel **reactor vessel** containing the **control rods** and the uranium fuel.

▶ This is the top of a nuclear reactor.

nuclear reactor   structure for making heat using radioactive substances

Controlling the speed

The control rods in a nuclear reactor control the speed of the reaction. If the control rods are lowered into the fuel, the reaction is slowed down.

Hot **coolant** comes out of the reactor. It is used to heat water and make steam.

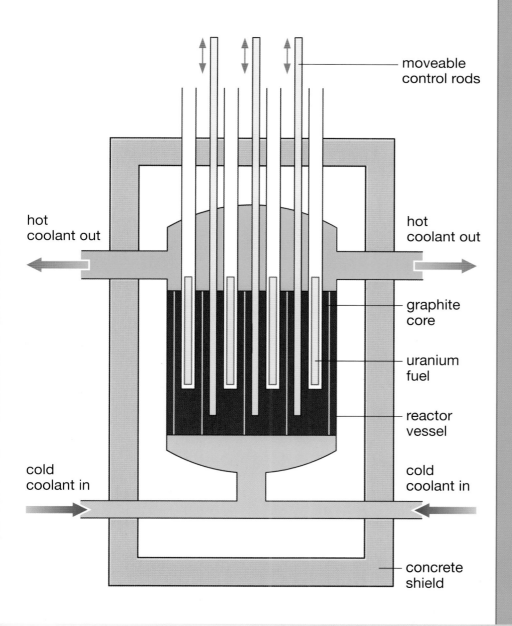

moveable control rods

hot coolant out

hot coolant out

graphite core

uranium fuel

reactor vessel

cold coolant in

cold coolant in

concrete shield

control rod   part of a nuclear reactor that controls the speed of the reaction

▲ The Calder Hall nuclear power station in 1957.

The first nuclear power station

The first nuclear power station in the world was built at Calder Hall in northwestern England. It was opened in 1956. It closed down in 2003 because it was too expensive to run.

There is a lot of **radiation** left at the site. It will take 100 years to make the site safe again.

▶ The hot water in a nuclear power station is cooled using huge cooling towers like these.

Mining uranium

A lot of the world's **uranium** comes from Australia. The rest of the world's uranium comes from Kazakhstan, Canada, South Africa, and Namibia.

▲ This is a uranium mine in Australia.

uranium   radioactive metal used as a fuel

Using Nuclear Power

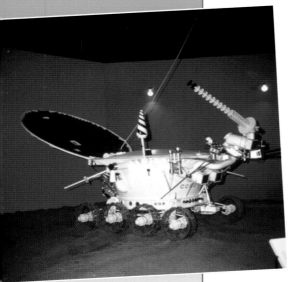

We have seen how nuclear **energy** can be used to make electricity. But nuclear energy has lots of other uses. For example, many spacecraft use nuclear energy to work their computers and other equipment.

Nuclear power in space

Some spacecraft have small **nuclear reactors**. They use these to make electricity.

Keeping warm on the Moon

This is a Russian Moon **rover**. It was kept warm on the Moon by nuclear power.

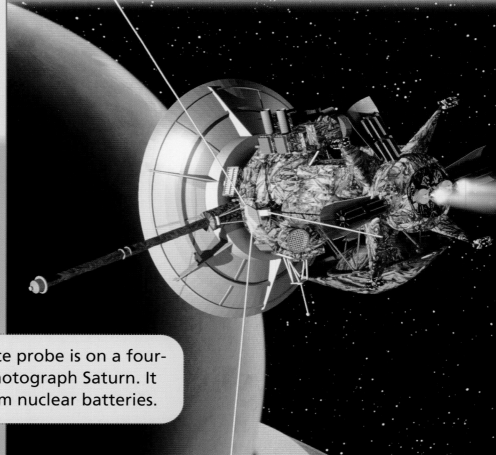

▶ The Cassini space probe is on a four-year mission to photograph Saturn. It gets its power from nuclear batteries.

Word Store　　rover　moving machine for collecting information about a planet or moon

Nuclear batteries

Other spacecraft have nuclear batteries. The batteries change the heat energy provided by the **radioactive** metal plutonium into electricity.

Nuclear batteries are small and easy to carry in a spacecraft. They also last for a very long time. This is useful in space because some missions last many years.

▼ This picture shows a spacecraft crashing toward Earth.

Spacecraft crashes

Spacecraft with radioactive substances can be dangerous if they crash to Earth. They might spread radioactive substances over a huge area.

Nuclear power at sea

Another useful place to use nuclear power is at sea. Most nuclear ships have two small **nuclear reactors** on board.

Nuclear ships only need refueling every ten years.

▼ This is the USS *Enterprise*, the world's first nuclear-powered aircraft carrier. It was launched in 1961.

Pushing through ice

The picture above shows two nuclear submarines at the North Pole.

Problems with nuclear ships

Nuclear ships cost a lot of money to build. They also cost a lot to run.

Many countries do not like nuclear-powered ships in their ports. They will only let them in after a lot of safety checks have been carried out.

Icebreakers

This is a nuclear-powered **icebreaker**. Icebreakers are very powerful ships that can break through pack ice.

icebreaker ship that can move through ice on the surface of the sea

Nuclear Problems

Nuclear power stations make less than one-fifth of the world's electricity. Nearly all the rest comes from power stations that burn **fossil fuels.**

Fossil fuels can damage the environment. They give out a gas called carbon dioxide when they burn. Carbon dioxide traps heat close to Earth. Many people think that this is causing **global warming.**

Carbon dioxide levels

The graph shows how the amount of carbon dioxide is increasing. This is because of the increased burning of fossil fuels.

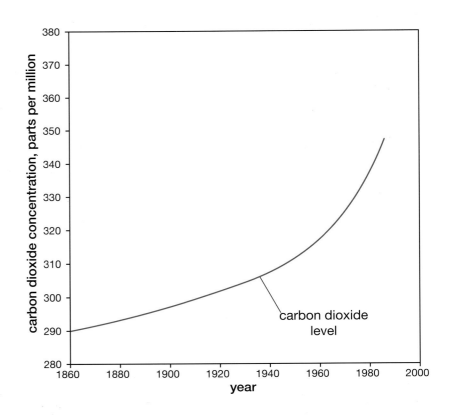

carbon dioxide level

global warming   extra warming of Earth caused by an increased greenhouse effect

A nuclear future?

Nuclear power does not cause global warming. Some people believe that we should make more electricity using **nuclear reactors**. But nuclear power does cause problems.

▼ Burning fossil fuels damages the environment.

Nuclear electricity

This bar chart shows how much electricity is made by nuclear power stations in the US, UK, and France.

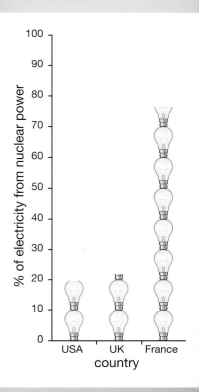

Problems with nuclear energy

The main problem with nuclear **energy** is the dangerous **radiation** caused by **radioactive** materials.

When a nuclear power station is closed down, the **reactor** is carefully taken apart. Most of the radioactive material is buried deep underground.

A blue glow

Most used nuclear fuel is stored in water for several years. The cooling pond glows blue (below).

Used fuel

Some parts of used **fuel** can be used again to make new fuel. But the **waste** material left behind has to be dealt with carefully.

Radioactive waste stays radioactive for thousands of years. Scientists have to think very carefully about where to dispose of it.

Nuclear protests

Many people are unhappy about nuclear power and radioactive waste. These people are protesting about nuclear power in France.

◄ These metal containers of radioactive waste will be buried underground.

Nuclear accidents

Things can go wrong at nuclear power stations. Then there is a big danger that **radioactive** substances will escape.

The Chernobyl disaster

In 1986, scientists were doing an experiment in a nuclear power station near Chernobyl in the Ukraine. It went badly wrong. The **nuclear reaction** went out of control.

Three Mile Island

In 1979, an accident occurred at the Three Mile Island nuclear power station in Pennsylvania. Dangerous radiation leaked out of the reactor. Robots (above) had to be used in the cleanup.

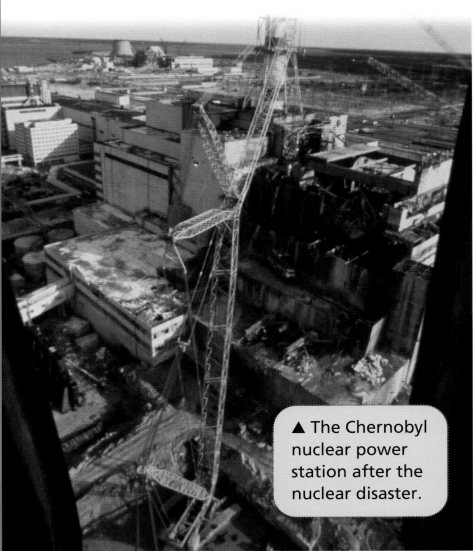

▲ The Chernobyl nuclear power station after the nuclear disaster.

There was an explosion. It blew off the top of the **nuclear reactor**. The **reactor core** caught fire. Huge amounts of radioactive substances escaped.

Cleaning up

It took several days to put out the fires in the Chernobyl reactor. Over 4,000 of the cleanup workers died from the effects of **radiation**.

▼ Pripyat is a town near the wrecked Chernobyl reactor. No one is allowed to live there today.

Nuclear Fusion

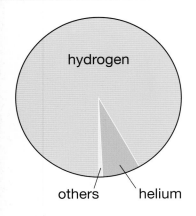

hydrogen

others   helium

The Sun

The Sun is made up of hydrogen atoms, helium atoms, and other atoms. The pie chart above shows the amounts of different atoms in the Sun.

There is a second way of making nuclear **energy**. It is called **nuclear fusion**. The word fusion means joining together.

In nuclear fusion, two small **atoms** hit each other very hard. Their **nuclei** join together. This makes the **nucleus** bigger and gives off **radiation** energy.

▼ The Sun's energy is provided by nuclear fusion.

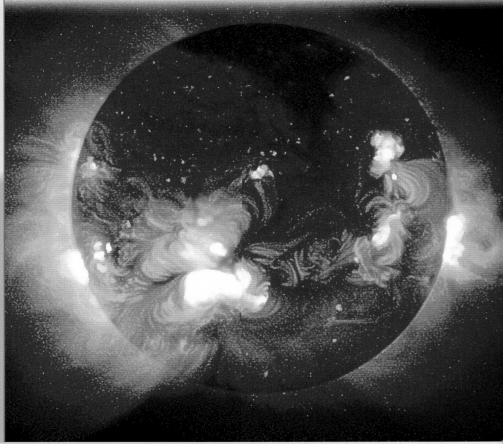

nuclear fusion   nuclear reaction where the nuclei of two atoms join together

Nuclear fusion in the Sun

The Sun is a star. All the stars gain their energy from nuclear fusion. The Sun is like a gigantic nuclear explosion happening in the sky.

Supernova

A supernova (left) is the explosion that happens when a star reaches the end of its life.

Nuclear fusion on Earth

Scientists are looking for a way to carry out **nuclear fusion**. The **energy** produced would solve a lot of the world's energy problems.

At the moment, nuclear fusion is not safe to do on Earth. So far we have only used nuclear fusion to make atomic bombs.

Atomic bombs

Nuclear fusion is used to make atomic bombs. This huge crater in the Nevada Desert, was made by an atomic bomb in 1962.

Electricity from nuclear fusion

It will be very difficult and very expensive to find a way to use nuclear fusion. Very high temperatures are needed to heat the fuel. Our **nuclear reactors** would be destroyed by these high temperatures.

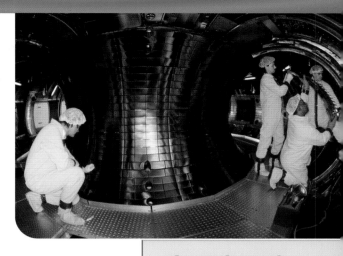

The tokamak

Scientists use a machine called a tokamak in their experiments with nuclear fusion. It is shaped like a hollow doughnut (above).

▼ Many people do not agree with nuclear weapons. This picture shows a protest against them.

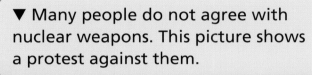

The Future of Nuclear Power

Nuclear power has both benefits and problems.

The benefits

Nuclear power stations are easy to run. They produce a large amount of **energy** from a very small amount of **fuel**.

Nuclear power does not cause **global warming**. If **nuclear fusion** can be made to work on Earth, we would have enough energy to last forever.

Laser fusion

The nuclear fusion reaction can be started with **lasers** (below).

Word Store   laser   beam of concentrated light or heat energy

The problems

The main problem with nuclear power is **radioactive waste**. This stays dangerous for a very long time. Some waste will still be dangerous in 250,000 years' time.

Nuclear power stations do not often go wrong, but if they do the results can be very serious.

There is only enough **uranium** on Earth to last about 65 years. Once we have used it, it will be gone forever.

◄ This is a French **nuclear reactor**. It had to be closed down because of leaks.

Find Out More

Organizations

The ABCs of Nuclear Science

The ABCs of Nuclear Science is a bright and colorful introduction to Nuclear Science. Learn how elements on Earth were produced. Discover if there are **radioactive** products found in a grocery store. Find out if you have ever eaten radioactive food. The ABCs of Nuclear Science welcomes your comments and questions. Contact them at the following address:
Mail Stop 70-319
Lawrence Berkeley
National Laboratory
Berkeley, CA 94720

Books

Energy for Life: Nuclear Energy, Robert Snedden (Heinemann Library, 2002)
Science Topics: Energy, Chris Oxlade (Heinemann Library, 2000)

World Wide Web

To find out more about nuclear energy, you can search the Internet using keywords like these:

- nuclear +[name of country]
- "nuclear fission"
- "nuclear fusion"
- "nuclear power"
- "nuclear reactor"
- radiation
- radioactivity
- uranium +fuel
- Chernobyl +nuclear

You can find your own keywords by using words from this book. The search tips opposite will help you find the most useful web sites.

Search tips

There are billions of pages on the Internet. It can be difficult to find exactly what you are looking for. These tips will help you find useful web sites more quickly:

- Know what you want to find out about.
- Use simple keywords.
- Use two to six keywords in a search.
- Only use names of people, places, or things.
- Put double quote marks around words that go together, for example "nuclear energy" or "nuclear fission"

Where to search

Search engine

A search engine looks through millions of web site pages. It lists all the sites that match the words in the search box. You will find the best matches are at the top of the list, on the first page.

Search directory

A person instead of a computer has sorted a search directory. You can search by keyword or subject and browse through the different sites. It is like looking through books on a library shelf.

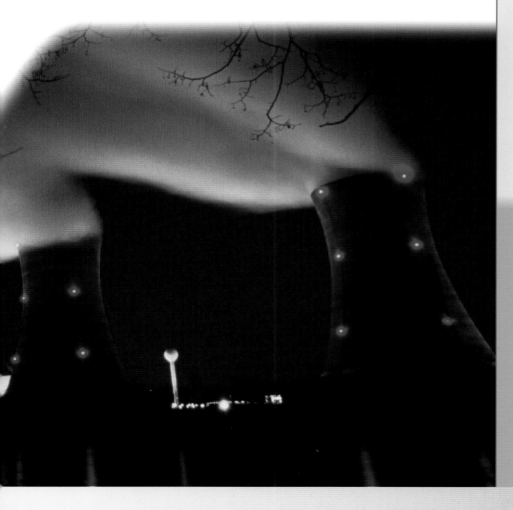

Glossary

atom tiny particle. Everything is made from atoms.

bacteria tiny organisms that can harm the body

cancer disease caused by cells growing out of control

cell tiny object that living things are made from

chain reaction nuclear reaction that keeps itself going

control rod part of a nuclear reactor that controls the speed of the reaction

coolant gas or liquid that takes the heat away from the reactor core

DNA chemical that carries information that cells need to work properly

electron tiny particle found in atoms

energy being able to do work. Light, heat, and electricity are types of energy.

fossil fuel coal, oil, or natural gas

fuel substance that stores energy and releases it when it is burned

fuel rod rods of nuclear fuel that are used in nuclear power stations

generator equipment used to make electricity

geothermal anything to do with heat from deep underground

global warming extra warming of Earth caused by an increased greenhouse effect

icebreaker ship that can move through ice on the surface of the sea

laser beam of concentrated light or heat energy

nuclear fission splitting atoms

nuclear fusion nuclear reaction where the nuclei of two atoms join together

nuclear reaction reaction that changes the nucleus of an atom

nuclear reactor structure for making heat using radioactive substances

nuclei more than one nucleus

nucleus center of an atom

particle tiny bit of something

particle accelerator machine that speeds up subatomic particles to very high speeds

radiation type of energy in the form of rays, waves, or particles

radioactive something that can give off radiation

ray beam of light or radiation

reactor core main part of a nuclear reactor

reactor vessel container for the reactor core

rover moving machine for collecting information about a planet or moon

subatomic particles tiny bits that make up atoms

turbine machinery that is turned by moving air, water, or steam

ultraviolet radiation form of light that is not visible to the eye

uranium radioactive metal used as a fuel

waste unwanted material left behind

Index